Lucas and Emily's Animal Adventure

Written by
Dave Grunenwald

Illustrated by
Bonnie Lemaire

Halo
PUBLISHING
INTERNATIONAL

Halo Publishing International
7550 WIH-10 #800, PMB 2069,
San Antonio, TX 78229

First Edition, August 2023
ISBN: 978-1-63765-414-9
Library of Congress Control Number: 2023907446

Halo Publishing International is a self-publishing company that publishes adult fiction and non-fiction, children's literature, self-help, spiritual, and faith-based books. Do you have a book idea you would like us to consider publishing? Please visit www.halopublishing.com for more information.

This book is dedicated to grandparents and grandchildren around the world.

Thanks for the assistance of my daughters Jill Grunenwald and Amy Burke, and that of my associate Terry Stephens.

4

Lucas inquires, "Grandma, could you tell me what a merit badge is?"

She responds, "It's a form of reward for accomplishing something enjoyable. The Grandparent Merit Badges serve as an inspiration for activities we can do together."

Lucas proceeds to flip through the badges, and before long, his grandparents and he begin planning their adventures.

ZOO

Lucas asks his grandma, "Can we go somewhere fun and see some new things together today?"

His grandma responds, "Absolutely, Lucas. Where would you like to go?"

Grandpa suggests, "How about we go on a bike ride to the zoo and the aquarium? We can make it an animal adventure!"

Excitedly, Lucas replies, "Yes! Let's invite my friend Emily and see if she can come along too."

Grandma and Grandpa smile at each other in agreement.

ART
SUPPLiES

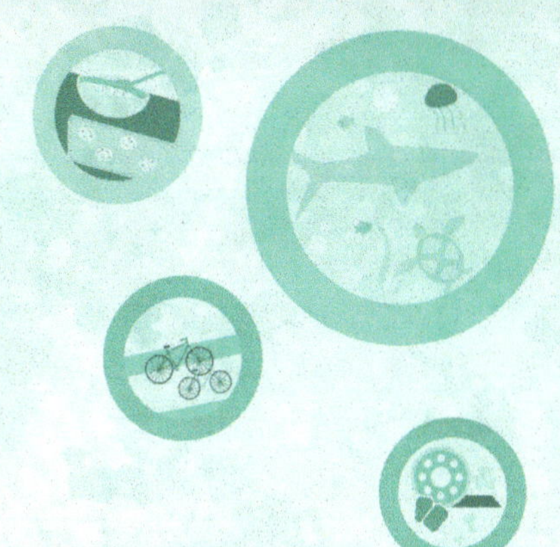

"Lucas, let's create a map of our exciting adventure!" exclaims Grandma.

"Wow, that's a wonderful idea, Grandma! It'll be twice the fun with Emily," replies Lucas, jumping up and down with excitement.

"All right, let me grab some paper and colored pencils," says Grandpa. "We'll draw on our map all the spots we want to visit," he adds, eagerly joining in on the fun.

Zoo
AQUARIUM

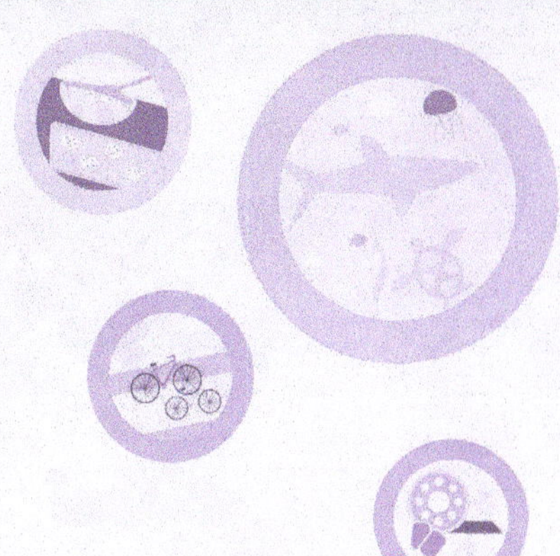

"Let's put your house in this corner, and don't forget to put Emily's house here," Grandma says while pointing.

"The aquarium goes here, and the zoo goes there," Grandpa says as he points too.

Lucas remarks, "The aquarium and the zoo are near each other, so we can all ride our bikes to the aquarium and walk to the zoo. This will be fun."

Zoo
AQUARIUM

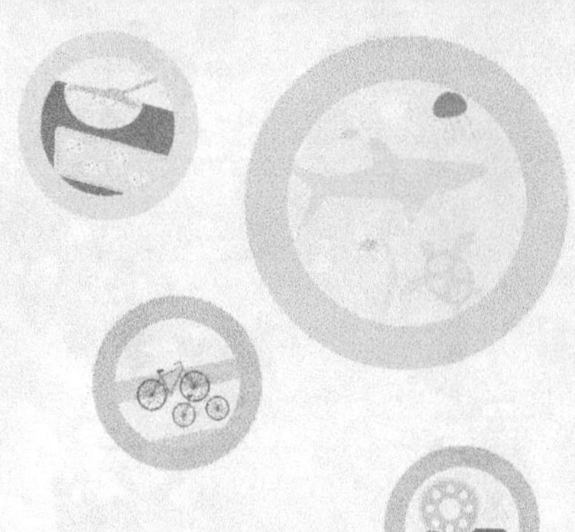

"Think of all the things we can do together another day," Grandpa says, still looking at the merit badges. "Next time, we can go to the park to fish and then fly a kite!" he adds.

"There are all kinds of merit badges we can earn," says Lucas, looking through the kit. "There's cooking, art projects, and other fun stuff too—we can have a whole series of adventures. Maybe our next activity can be an outdoor adventure."

Grandma asks Lucas, "Are you ready for our animal adventure?"

"Oh yes, this is going to be such a fun day," he responds.

"The aquarium and the zoo, both in one day," says Grandpa.

"We can't wait," shouts Lucas as Emily nods in agreement.

"Look at that beautiful sunshine," says Lucas. "Grandma and Grandpa, I love hanging out with you," he adds. "It's going to be a wonderful day."

"Thanks for inviting me. I've never been to the zoo," Emily says.

"Emily, I am glad you could come. I especially like going on adventures with a friend along too," Lucas replies.

Entering the aquarium, Emily's and Lucas's eyes open wide.

"Wow, look at the sharks. The jellyfish too," Emily remarks. "Those sharks have such big teeth. The fish are yellow, blue, and green," she adds, "and are striped and spotted too!"

"Let's find the tunnel. It's my favorite part," Lucas says.

Grandpa asks Lucas, "What is your favorite sea creature at the aquarium?"

"I'll have to think a bit about that because there are so many," Lucas responds.

"I really like the octopi and the turtles," says Emily. "They are such different shapes."

"Octopi? What's an oc-to-pi?" asks Lucas.

"It's what you say when there is more than one octopus," answers Emily.

"It sounds like a dessert to me... I'm hungry." Lucas laughs. "Do you think fish get hungry like we do?"

As they walk through the tunnel and are looking up, the kids exclaim, "Wow!"

"Look at the school of stingrays swimming overhead," says Lucas.

Emily begins counting, "One...two...three...four...five...six...seven!"

"I like the way they stay together and seem to fly as a group," Grandpa says. "They look very majestic."

Lucas agrees and says, "Let's go through the tunnel again."

As they continue their journey, Lucas asks, "Do you think we can feed the sharks?"

"Yes, I am sure we can," says Grandpa. Pointing, he adds, "We can buy shark food right over there."

"Let's buy some food and find a good spot near the tank," Grandma says.

BEARS
LIONS
26

"The aquarium has been great," says Lucas.

"Let's walk over to the zoo now," Grandma says.

"Good idea, Grandma," Lucas responds. "We've seen the animals underwater. Now, we're going to see those on land as well."

As they approach the zoo, Grandma and Grandpa ask the kids, "What is your favorite part of the zoo?"

"Lions and tigers and bears!" Lucas shouts.

Grandma and Grandpa look at each other, and Grandma replies, "Oh my!"

Emily has never been to the zoo, so she asks Lucas, "Do you like snakes?"

"I think so. They are beautiful, but a little bit scary," Lucas replies as he feigns fright with his facial expression.

"It's okay; they are in glass cages, so let's have a look at them," says Grandpa. "Look, here is one laying eggs!"

ELEPHANT
GIRAFFE

After looking at the snakes, they continue their journey to the outside exhibits.

"I like the elephants," says Emily. "They are like giants with those big ears. I wonder if they can fly," she adds.

Lucas then says that giraffes are even taller and seem to touch the sky. "Look how they eat the leaves off of the trees!" he adds.

MONKEYS
TiGers
32

"Let's visit the building where the lions and tigers and cheetahs live," says Grandma. "It is new this year, and there are a great many other animals in there too."

Grandpa asks, "Have you ever seen a white tiger?"

"Did you say a white tiger?! I didn't know that tigers can be white. I thought they were striped or spotted," Emily says as Lucas nods his head.

Excitement is in the air.

As they leave the zoo, Grandpa says, "It is time to head home."

"Thanks for inviting me," says Emily. "It's been a wonderful day."

"Grandpa, when we get home, can we fill out the pages for visiting the zoo and the aquarium in your kit, and then plan our outdoor adventure?" Lucas asks.

"Of course. Next time, we'll take Jack with us. There is still lots more to do," Grandpa says.

To be continued...